A Mama for Owen

SIMON & SCHUSTER BOOKS FOR YOUNG READERS
An imprint of Simon & Schuster Children's Publishing Division
1230 Avenue of the Americas, New York, New York 10020
Text copyright © 2007 by Marion Dane Bauer
Illustrations copyright © 2007 by John Butler
All rights reserved, including the right of reproduction in whole or in part in any form.
SIMON & SCHUSTER BOOKS FOR YOUNG READERS is a trademark of Simon & Schuster, Inc.
Book design by Lucy Ruth Cummins
The text for this book is set in Cinnamon.
The illustrations for this book are rendered in acrylic paint and colored pencils.
Manufactured in China
2 4 6 8 10 9 7 5 3 1
Library of Congress Cataloging-in-Publication Data
Bauer, Marion Dane.
A mama for Owen / written by Marion Dane Bauer ; illustrated by John Butler.— 1st ed.
p. cm.
Summary: When the 2004 Indian Ocean tsunami separates a young African hippopotamus from his mother,
he finds a new snuggle partner in Mzee the giant tortoise. Based on a true story.
ISBN-13: 978-0-689-85787-4
ISBN-10: 0-689-85787-X
1. Hippopotamus—Juvenile fiction. [1. Hippopotamus—Fiction. 2. Turtles—Fiction. 3. Parental behavior in animals—Fiction.
4. Indian Ocean Tsunami, 2004. 5. Tsunamis—Fiction.] I. Butler, John, 1952- ill. II. Title
PZ10.3.B317Mam 2007
[E]—dc22 2005034364

A Mama for Owen

By Marion Dane Bauer
Illustrated by John Butler

Simon & Schuster Books for Young Readers
New York   London   Toronto   Sydney

Owen was a very young hippo.

He lived with his mother, his father, his aunts,
and his cousins in the Sabaki River in Africa.

Owen loved the river.
But even more he loved his great grayish brown—or was she
brownish gray?—mama.
Every day Owen and his mama slept together.
They swam together.
They ate together.

Even when Mama left the river to graze in the moonlight, Owen followed close behind her stubby tail.

Best of all, Owen loved to play hide-and-seek.

Mama hid and Owen found her.

And every time he found his mama, he licked her friendly face,
laid his head on her broad back, and smiled his great pink smile.

But all that was before
the rain began to fall.

The rain fell
and it fell
and it fell.
The Sabaki River rose
and it rose
and it rose.
The river ran faster
and faster
and faster.
The river rose so high
and ran so fast
that it washed
Owen
and his mother
and his father
and his aunts
and his cousins
all the way out to sea.

Owen roared for his mama, but his mama did not answer.
He roared louder. No Mama!
He searched and searched, but his mama wasn't hiding.
She was lost.
And Owen was alone in the sea.

He roared and roared and roared until finally he lost even his roar.

And that was when the great wave came and washed Owen back to shore.

Owen was befuddled and weak and very, very sad.
He looked all around this new place. This wasn't his river!
He looked around some more. Where was his mama?

Then Owen saw . . . something brownish gray.

Or was it grayish brown?

He wasn't sure.

But he staggered over and snuggled down next to it.

And the very old tortoise, whose name was Mzee,
lay very still while Owen waited for sleep to come.

When Owen woke, he looked again at the tortoise.
Mzee was colored just like his mama. Mzee was large just like his mama.
Mzee had stayed very close when Owen needed him . . .
just like his mama used to do.

Owen laid his head on Mzee's broad back and slept some more.

Now Owen and Mzee sleep together.
They swim together.
They eat together.

Whenever Mzee goes for a walk, moonlight or sunlight,
Owen follows close behind his stubby tail.

Owen's favorite game is still hide-and-seek.

Mzee slips beneath the water, and Owen plunges in to find him.
Mzee nestles in the long grass,
and Owen peers through the grass until he spots him.

Mzee rests behind a rock, and Owen searches and searches until . . .

There is Mzee!

And whenever Mzee takes a nap, tucked away inside his
brownish gray—or is it grayish brown?—shell,
Owen waits
and waits
and waits
until he can find Mzee once more.

Then when he finds Mzee, Owen licks his friendly face, lays his head on the tortoise's broad back, and smiles his great pink smile.

Author's Note

The story of Owen and a giant tortoise named Mzee, which means "old man" in Swahili, is a true one. Owen was rescued by the Kenya Wildlife Service and local fishermen after the hippopotamus and his family were washed down the Sabaki River by a flood and he was brought back to shore by a tsunami wave. Owen was less than a year old—hippopotamus calves ordinarily stay with their mothers for four years—and no one could find his mother. So they brought him to Haller Park, a nature preserve outside of Mombasa. There the lonely young hippo chose Mzee, a 130-year-old male tortoise, to be his mother; and Mzee doesn't seem to mind one little bit.